K

A Collection of Poetry

Kaleidoscope:

A Collection of Poetry

Christine Routledge

Paper Doll

© Christine Routledge 1998

Published by Paper Doll
Belasis Hall
Coxwold Way
Billingham
Cleveland

ISBN: 1 86248 072 9

Typeset by CBS, Felixstowe, Suffolk
Printed by Lintons Printers, Co. Durham

To my family and friends

With Best Wishes from Christine Routledge

CONTENTS

Enchantment	1
Sonnet	2
Blue Flight	3
Oak Tree	4
Blackbird	5
Fish	6
Dawn On The Roof - Spain	8
Scotland	9
Prayer	10
Deer In the Dark	11
Alcazabar Spain	12
Nevis	13
Cottle Church	14
Seer	15
Peer Gynt	16
Returning To London	17
Hither Green Lane	18
Love	19
To Part	20
Night	21
Doorway	23
Dream	24
Self Pity	25
Rodent	26
Persona And Self	27
Unprovoked Attack At Work	28
The Mask	29
Possibilities	31

Why?	32
Insanity	34
Hymn	35
Greenwich Park	37
The End	38
Dance Of Life	39
Anubis	40
Heat Wave In May	41
Dawn	42
The Moon	43
The River	44
Haiku Poems (Eltham)	47
Haiku Poems (Venezuela)	48
Two Views Of The Same Event:	
1. Romantic View	49
2. Realistic View	50
Them	51
Teddy Bear	52
Another Glass Of Wine?	53
You	54
Monument	55
Once I Was Able To Sit Upon Your Knee	56
Dad	57
The Purple Bamboo Park (A Glimpse Of Heaven)	58
Thassos	60
Animal Farm	61

ENCHANTMENT

Upon the softly lapping water
That time alone changes or mars,
Float waterlilies; each a tiny altar
Offering its beauty to the distant stars.
Nature's scented jewels, purifying and perfuming,
Lie scattered near the banks
And the willow sweeps into the clear water,
Its branches like long hanks
Of hair. The moon softly illuminates
With a mellow light the emerald green
And time seems suspended – time waits,
Beauty is here as in a dream.

But just as a dream the enchantment fades,
Intangible and frail, elusive as a mirage,
It has gone.
But slowly rejuvenated, a new magic takes its place,
A distant light, a distinct song,
And numerous fairy-like dragonflies which trace
Intricate patterns over the shimmering water.
As day breaks a thread of golden ray
Shines across those enchanted waters
To mark the beginning of a new day.

SONNET

The golden sun sets slowly in the skies,
A radiant ball, a brilliant glow
Of fiery red which slowly sinks below
The horizon and the day softly dies.
First comes uncertain twilight, then the night
With the rising of the silvery moon,
And stars across the velvet sky are strewn,
Tiny pinpoints of bright celestial light,
Making shimmery the gnarled old tree.
And all is still and silent as the grave,
The silence seeming to embalm and bathe
The town in a cloak of tranquillity.
All is peaceful and safe as in a dream
Humanity sleeps, and nature's supreme.

BLUE FLIGHT

Bird in the blue, swift winged motion,
Soul stirring to express the ecstasy
Of the dark cool glades,
Impenetrable by the thrust,
The intensity of light.
The marigolds and sunflowers
Burning, consuming the light,
The cottage half in shadow.
And the beach, the putrid flesh sizzled
Lax and languid, the vitality
Cannot penetrate the soul.
All are in the bird in the blue
Singleness of motion, cleaving, swooping
In the fathomless blue.
And the bird within me swoons,
To break through the bars –
To be at one with the bird in the blue.
And I am that bird.

Piercing, searing the translucent blue
The aerial molecules part and yield
Before the momentous ecstasy of flight.

OAK TREE

Green avenues shade the sloping road
That leads to the city of confusion,
While etched in tracery
My leaves quiver
Ecstatic to a blue world
Fleeced with dreams of milk.

Swaying in the warmth
Of balmy summer breezes,
Integral with the vital sun
That dapples me in gold,
I feel the knowledge deep in my dark heart
It rises with the sap.

I am indifferent to the lad that shins me,
The couple that shelter with their love
Beneath my gnarled canopy,
And birds that flutter endlessly
Through my spreading branches,
For my roots reach deep
Even to the grave
Drawing moisture.

BLACKBIRD

Blackbird,
Dull jade nestled in lattice branches
Flashing gem in the vital sun,
Cleaving the heights
In instinct of joy,
Shimmering world of green and grey
Beyond conception.

Until some child
In careless spite
Against your wild bright joy
Shot you, fluttering down,
No more embrace the wild wide wind.

Blackbird,
A huddled mass of rags now
Tremble, quiver in young alien grasp
And weary, drained, passive,
Prepare to soar that last bare mountain
Instinct told you of so long ago.

FISH

Fish darts pure
Ray of light
Shining pool
Fins on fire
Free.

Cruel hook poised
Pant last pang
Eyes fixed stare
Sparkle fades
Caught.

Child's hand
Stirs the water
Draws a pebble
From the brook
And bright fish swims
Through tangled roots
Of withered tree
As Summer's haze
Fades away
Bathed in evening mist.

Desert tree
Roots blanched
Searing sun
Withered leaves
Drying.
Arid land

Beetle scuttles
Great tree sighs
Dying.

DAWN ON THE ROOF – SPAIN

Quiet waters lapping
On pale deserted beaches.
The wind prancing through
The waves of bloated bulrushes.
And crickets silenced
As the oyster shell cracks open wide
The mystery of dawn's pale glimmer.

And now,
Here above the world
I raise my arms in silent greeting
As the sun emerges
From the hazy mountains,
And vague fishing boats return
Like guests unto the silent watchers.

SCOTLAND

A star pierced bright and made me pause
By foaming blades of flame.
My arms outstretched, I reabsorbed
The phoenix in my heart. And man that asked,
I cannot tell if I am spirit, or beast or bird,
Or wind and sky together.

PRAYER

Wind in my hair
I am at one with you,
Grass beneath my feet
Convey me.
Rainbow in my eyes
And stream in my heart
Retain me.

Birds arising like a dart
Over stubble of corn
Take me too;
And air embrace me
Like a leaf.
In pure light
Keep me.

DEER IN THE DARK

Treading invisible through the gloom
We sense each other's wildness.
A flicker of freedom binds us
Like a tongue of fire
And we will not lose our way
For the stars will be our eyes,
And the close and secret dark
The thread which finds us.

ALCAZABAR SPAIN

Dragonfly, transparent, vital spark,
Ember of the sun
Hovers over lily pond
Dense with fairy boats
And darting fish of gold.

The ancient walls watch,
Jealously protecting a timeless secret,
And Arabic terraces of cacti spears
Await the silent consummation
Of a legend.

A mirage in the haze conceived
Of Moorish maiden by the pond
Holding dragonfly with laughter
Dark and old as the earth itself.

I stand here and yet
I am not within this dream,
Nor can I capture it with word or camera.
But feel within a past
Without thought. Without word
That accepts and will not analyse
All that is the dragonfly,
The secret of Alcazabar,
All that is.

NEVIS

The sea gently laps on a distant shore
So many miles from home;
The sun is a demon dancing hot
In the cauldron of an azure sky
Fleeced with cauliflower clouds.
Charcoal bodies drift in and out
Of the warm still waters,
And calypso music casually wafts
Across the peaceful bay.
A little speedboat swiftly ploughs
Skimming the turquoise waves
To the hazy vista of islands beyond the horizon.
And prehistoric-looking pelicans fish
Like darts beyond black volcanic rocks,
As the palm fronds gaily dance
In the cooling trade winds,
Make a music of their own.

And my spirit is refreshed
And bathed in the golden light
Of this little Caribbean isle.

COTTLE CHURCH

In the silent stillness
Of a waist-high tropical grassland
Hardly a lizard moved,
And the sun's fires blazed relentlessly.
There, almost reclaimed by the forest,
Shrouded in verdant growth
A few stones valiantly stood
Survivors of an earthquake,
Giving echoes of a less peaceful past
When our dark-skinned shackled brothers
Walked with their fair skinned masters,
Stood together, and raised their voices
In unison to God.

Now, the quiet solitude
Where once the sound of long skirts rustled,
Scriptures boomed out and music radiated
Through open windows and doors.
And yet these stones were never hallowed
By the corrupt, dispassionate clergy,
And were perhaps shunned by other masters,
Surrounded by ignorance and mistrust.

But how peaceful now the ruins are,
And how healed the hurt
With wreaths of green.

SEER

On the edge of an overhanging rock
The prophet stood
His arms outstretched in the golden light,
Pure eyes shining clear and bright,
And love was all he was and knew.

PEER GYNT

Crack the walnut's hard protective shell
And find inside the sweet white kernels,
And peel the onion skin and ring upon ring
Until you reach the heart.
And invite true friends, like knights of old
With words not maces, lances, swords and shafts,
To ambush the grim and ponderous castle
And tear down brick upon brick
Of lies, deceit, and self-delusion
And so rescue the lonely soul walled deep within.

RETURNING TO LONDON

Back to the haunted tunnel, reverberating voids,
Back to the hard metallic cranes
That rip the sombre sky,
To the pale desolate streets lacking vitality,
That echo with the footsteps close behind.

Back also to the grey silent shadows
Where huddled outcasts spit life's blood
With phlegm from broken lungs.
Returning to a lie in a city of shame;
To a noisy hell permeated by the gloom
Of being alone.

Returning once more to London,
To the cold bleak monuments
Corrupting a condemned sky,
And to the bridges stretched out like worms
Over a dead and tortuous river
That pulsates its concrete banks
Hoping for revenge.

HITHER GREEN LANE

Metal grating on metal
A high-pitched tooth edging sound,
An argument below,
Voices spitting out vehemence
And Radio One intermittently
Spewing out trivia.
Enjoy the peace.

The tin roof of a factory
Corrugation peeling off.
A puddle that shrinks, and expands
After each successive cloudburst.
A brick wall variegated
With sickly yellow and grey.
And yes! If you crane your neck
You can just about see
The gradually clouding blue,
The billowing dry-cleaning fumes
Temporarily obscuring sight.
So if you come and visit me
Do admire the view!

My heart is filled with sorrow and pain
Why came I hither to this ungreen lane?

LOVE

You have trod the halls of Valhalla
With glittering moonstones in your hair,
In star lit robes of fantasy
You wove the web of life;
With butterfly wings you painted an exotic sky
And threw joyful sequins at the sullen night.
In slow ecstatic movements
You have been the dancer,
Trailing streamers gay with laughter.
You have been sorrow,
And you have been the harlequin.
You have been the thousand patterns
In a rainbowed kaleidoscope;
And the hundredth name the camel knows.

You have been all.
You have been nothing.
I think they called you Love.

TO PART

I did not know how much I loved
Until I saw the empty bustle
And faces blank, a stiff smile,
Dressmakers' dummies.
Smiling at each other – not knowing
What to say;
Unemotional, blithe,
'Don't do anything I wouldn't do,'
Pathetic afterthought,
'You will write, won't you?'
When really what the tender heart
Longs to express
Are the whispered words
'I love you.'
'God protect you – don't forget me.'
Oh, if we could break the barrier of flesh,
The trite phrases,
And say what really mattered.
But I can say little,
I cannot even see through
The veil of tears,
You smile, and wave goodbye.

NIGHT

The grey shadows lengthen slowly
And dark spaces engulf the pools of light
Like sponges draining the vital colours,
And night, the jailor, treads relentlessly
Locking us in our solitary cells,
Prisoners of fear.

At night we tread the streets warily
Passing uncertain corners which harbour
Some nameless dread,
Hearing others' footsteps close behind,
Fearing some malicious intent;
Each self-contained in loneliness.
For in the night can brother know brother
Except for the light in their eyes?

And held closely in a lover's arms
There is still the dark between us
Creeping all around us;
The magician moon hotly burns our brows
With borrowed light peeps through the panes
Distorting the dancing shadows.
And doors and staircases creak and groan
As if some restless spirit wandered.

Night – the time the hunter stealthily stalks,
And the hunted cringes and hides,
Shrinking and inert.
Night – the time for the traitorous kiss

In the whispering garden;
The time for secret plans,
For cunning and disguise,
And for the scholars reading
Until the printed page jumps with their eyes,
Pens scratching out scrawly writing
Measuring the silent hours in cups of coffee.

Night – the time our star is hidden
And the light of stars of other worlds
Too weak to warm us.
Created in darkness, to darkness we return.
Each night we die, each day reborn.
Greeting the first shafts of light
Singing elegies to the dawn.

DOORWAY

Like a sleepwalker suddenly awakening
On a green world freshly created
I gaze around in wonder
With new born eyes that never really saw before.
Trying to absorb a medley of impressions,
Trying to find some pattern, some symbol,
A key to unlock the door.

Sometimes I am allowed to peep
Through a little chink in the door,
And then I feel the joy of being
Whole and perfect like a butterfly or bird.
And throwing open arms to the sky
I feel that I could really fly
Embracing the whole street
Skipping like a child along the lane
With so much happiness bursting inside
In joyful pain.

Perhaps one day I will remember
I have the key here in my hand,
And then the door will melt away
And I will understand.

DREAM

I dreamed of a new world created
A piercing voice singing in the sky,
And beautiful forms emerging
From swirling mist;
Everything bright, and pure and new.
I dreamed I awoke on that first dawn
To gaze around in wonder,
In joyful, happy innocence;
And I dreamed of a world filled
With love and caring, peace and harmony.

I dreamed of this planet earth
And everyone woke up.

SELF PITY

This day could have been a pearl
To set in a lighthouse
Guiding wandering mariners;
It could have been
A brightly painted butterfly
Flittering through the summer days,
It could have been a festival
Dancing through the streets,
Or baby's first innocent gaze.
I could have climbed Mount Everest
Or found the Philosopher's stone.

But I strangled it
In its conception,
It never had a chance.

RODENT

I saw a dead mouse once
From which huge worms were squirming.
The mouse's eyes were dead and dull,
His fur was like a brush,
They were white as leprosy and featureless,
But so many living from one dead.
And my scream was a silent panic;
Pandora should have kept that lid on tight.

PERSONA AND SELF

The persona walking in habitual blindness
Tripped over the self one day.
It whimpered, and timidly walked away
Like a wounded bird trying to hide
In some tangled undergrowth by the wayside.
There were many thorns and tough weeds
And the persona had a very hard job
To uncover it and draw it into the light.
Well, when it did, it stood and blinked a while
Then gaily spread its wings and flew
For joy in the flawless azure blue.

UNPROVOKED ATTACK AT WORK

Yes I am weak
And you mock me with your scorn
Like a sapling thrown down
By a violent storm.
I have no resistance
To your anger.
You hurt me, and abused me.
Why?

THE MASK

Veiled by the impenetrable facade
I try to strive through unyielding cobwebs
That bind me to the collective noun.

Let my eyes be but the windows of my soul
That I may evade that of me which is not
And offer at your shrine
That moiety which is
When that I know.
Thus in anguished contemplation,
Let my eyes reveal the raging depths of my
    passion.
And let me shatter
The medley impressions of impassive society
That swamp my aspirations.
Then if you are not afraid
Search the atom of my soul.
The elusive butterfly thronged
By the moths of frustration.
Tear, tear the iron flesh from these skeletal
    shackles,
Destroy the mask of ironical onlooker,
The fortress is not impregnable.
Await the moment my eyes are unguarded
Then seize the liquid being.

Can I not reveal
The secrets of my heart
Or is the mask still staid, impassive?

I long to communicate
To reach out – to let my consciousness flow
And combine with yours.
But inadequacy taunts me,
As from my mirror my reflection mocks me,
Impassive, amused, a name, a mask
That haunts me with the triteness, the trivia
Of concrete reality.
When my mind longs to escape, to unite,
And in my eyes is the message
Of my yearning
To be loved.

POSSIBILITIES

Like a weary traveller
Who having battled with the bitter wind and rain,
Peels off layers of clothing
And steams before the welcome fire,
So I, if I discard these pretences and lies,
May stand in the warmth of the sun
Free from life's desire.

WHY?

Aimlessly I wandered in a field of waving
    poppies
But their presence disturbed me
Writhing in scarlet madness
And I was afraid.

I walked along desolate beaches
And saw only ancient wrecks
Half submerged in silent caves
And perplexed, the question mark
Was washed by eternal greedy waves.

And I wandered through the graveyard,
Charnel house of life's aspirations
And rotten corpses trailing gnarled sinews
Stared with decaying eyeballs
Bouncing in hollow craniums,
But I do not see, for I am blind as they.

And I cried out
To the frozen wastes of the city,
Why?
But the ants stared in dumb incomprehension
And mechanically, umbrella, poised smile, red
    light
Paused. Dismissed. Continued.

And I cried out to my God
From the crystal halls
Of the mountains of the sun,
But only the teeming womb replied
Screeching a piercing song of light
And I did not understand.

INSANITY

Child, take my hand,
The dark clouds ride like crazed stallions
And iron hooves tattoo patterns in our heads.
The moon bleeds with every butcher's stab,
My child.
And the wind cleaves through our cobweb home
Scattering sand in our eyes.
Take my hand – we must flee
Through the trees that whisper menace
And the branches that whip our limbs.
We shall be engulfed in the mountains of the sea.
So let us flee my child
Before we are bleached white
Like a bone lying on a barren shore.

HYMN

And when I go, when
The last sand grain trickles
Through my wasted fingers;
When the north wind
Harshly extinguishes my flame,
And I a sighing breath
Lost in the blizzard, become
A shadow wandering desolate branches
Of precipitous mountain passes,
Who will be to feel the trees
Piercing the vastness of blue
Each branch quivering with the joy
Of the eternal moment?
Who will be to feel the bird
With outstretched wings caress
The soft pink sunset
Sinking into uncertain twilight?
And when I go
Who will watch the goldfish
Dart through pools of turquoise haze
Reflecting translucent pearls?
And marigolds that intensely tell
Of the burning secret of the sun?
And who will race at one with the wind,
Feel it teasing the springy branches,
Playfully eddying the swirls of dust?
And who then will be fulfilled
By the poppies blazing like madness
In fields of burnished gold?

And which knower will feel this moment,
Fill all space and time
With searing light?

GREENWICH PARK

Those endless summer days of childhood
Have long since gone
But the sun is still so bright and hot.
Sand passes through the glass
Far too quickly
Like ice melting in a warm room;
And we cling to the threads
Of memories, weaving our rich tapestries
Of life to wear around us
Should we begin to fear.
And the helpless baby and frail old lady
Are with me in my head
As I drink in the sunshine sitting on this hill
And prepare for winter.

THE END

This granite will not endure,
These cliffs will grind to sand,
And scattered in the wind
The ivory towers like paper cards will fly.
Rich man, your precious money will become
A handful of dry dust;
Lover, your body will fall to ash;
Preacher, your words will fall to silence;
Politician, your machinations will cease.
Yes, citizens, your proud citadels will crumble
The gigantic iridescent bubble will burst . . .
And
All
Will
Come
To
Rest
In
A
Core
Of
Stillness.

DANCE OF LIFE

We danced on the waves
That crested tomorrow
And we saw new horizons,
Stopping to sample their freshness
With lutes and lyres
On palm kissed beaches
We sang and clapped our hands.
We ate honey and ambrosia
And rode on unicorns
When Pegasus graced the sky.

Now there is a quietness
Of wave-lapping timelessness,
And we wait on the shore
Where question marks are erased.
And we smile, clasp hands
And dance in the light of the moon,
And here we wait
Until the ferryman should call us.

ANUBIS

In soniferous gaunt cathedrals lie
Armoured knights, fair ladies and their curs. Prone
On cold grey slabs, sad, solemn, and alone
Stilled for ever. On frozen lips their cry,
'This empty vault can never be our home.'
Deep the creeping gloom, dark the aisles and cold.

But far away in hazy arid land
An ancient sphinx rests on the desert sand,
Its steadfast gaze mystical secrets hold
Witness of when important men must die
How they build monuments to reach the sky,
Searing, gleaming white. Enter and be bold.

But I thought that burial tombs were not
Supposed to be like hell fires, flaring hot.

HEAT WAVE IN MAY

I longed for this moment of peace since dawn.
Released early from tedious toil I
Joyfully relax on buttercupped lawn,
The sun beams hotly in unblemished sky
Of azure blue. Piquant the blackbird's cry
To distant mate on tree, greetings windborne
While she placidly squats and incubates
Their eggs of porcelain, and calmly waits
His return from reconnaissance on high.
And I watch the garlanded horse chestnut trees
Dance to the rhythm of the subtle breeze
That cools my roasted limbs. I stretch and sigh,
Absorbed in the beauty of a perfect day.
So come, let's join hands and dance to the May.

DAWN

A shrouded moon trails
Wreaths of quietness
Across the weeping grass,
And the long cold hours
Of silent watching
Relax in the soft rebirth of dawn.
Gaunt grandfather trees emerge
From the mist.
Branches trembling in the crystalled air.
And a blackbird's distant cry
Softly echoed from aerial companions,
Greets a new dawn,
Capturing shafts of sunlight
On dreaming wings.

THE MOON

Only the vacant night gathered round
In silent unknown whispers,
And as I watched the lonely hill
The stars receded a hundred million miles away.

My thoughts echoed softly like
Drops of moisture in a cave, with
Only the trees for company.

These friends of old, I touched and knew
The sentinels of my soul,
Whispering deep secrets in the voice
Of the wind,
And telling of the ancient night,
Weaving webs of stillness
Around an esoteric moon.

THE RIVER

The beautiful river is born in the quiet loneliness
Of the distant hazy mountains.
A trickle of water issues through a rocky cleft
And dances sparkling in the sunshine
Leaping over the tiny pebbles and sudden drops
    and eddies,
And the eagle soars freely overhead
Wings kissing the pure light in joy.

Many little streams bound together in the valleys
To form one mighty river flowing ever onwards,
Past little harvest mice delicately balanced
On waving ears of golden corn,
Past cottage gardens – brief scent of lavender
    and honeysuckle,
Brief glance at prim hedges, and stately
    hollyhocks
And stiff starched washing waving in the breeze.
Past school boys patiently waiting with hook
    and line
And jam jars on strings,
And picnickers dangling naked feet
In the cool clear waters.
Home for the water boatman and pond skaters
Gaily skimming the surface,
Home for the jewelled fish swimming freely,
Home for the beavers, otters and voles,
Home for the birds chattering by the banks,
And for the kingfishers darting like

Sapphire in restless activity.

And slower, statelier, ever onwards
Across the plains towards the sea
It passes the allotments divided like a patchwork
Where men joyfully toil, wiping sweat
From brows with the backs of their hands,
And pause, and listen to its song.
It passes grim grey factories
Where the clanging machinery rings in the air,
And workgirls share their sandwiches
During a brief respite by its banks.

And through busy clamorous towns
Where living banks are hemmed by concrete walls,
Where the pigeons sit in line waiting to beg
From the townspeople,
And the sounds of traffic and loud voices
Almost drown the river's music.

And at last, with the tangy smell of salt and seaweed,
Bulrushes growing along the sedge,
And seagulls wheeling overhead,
The river meets its mother, the sea.

Ever flowing, ever travelling, always going
Yet always present.
Directionless, we find direction;
Asking nothing, we are given to understand.

One day, beautiful river, we also shall let go
And gently flow in your mighty heart
Like fallen petals.

HAIKU POEMS (ELTHAM)

Chilly dull evening,
Leaves cascading slowly down,
Cars crawling to town.

Evening chill, light fades,
Water ripples, traffic drones
Beyond verdant glades.

Little pond skaters skim,
The traffic drones on
And the light grows dim.

Endless traffic still,
Tuneful birds greet the evening,
Fish swim silently.

Leaves trailing above
And parading all around,
Carpeting the ground.

HAIKU POEMS (VENEZUELA)

Our small plane flew free
Fragile as a cardboard box
Tossed on a cruel sea.

Engine screeching loud,
Lurching, diving, swooping down,
Soaring through the cloud.

Waterfall so high
Cascading torrents falling.
(Please don't let us die!)

Craggy peaks above,
Wild verdant beauty below,
Suspended in between.

I must face my fear.
This terror will soon be gone;
Hold on, please hold on.

We landed at last
A primitive remote world,
Ageless, pure and vast.

TWO VIEWS OF THE SAME EVENTS

1. Romantic view:

Standing by the water's edge
Lit by the embers of a sunset
You pointed happily at a little yellow hammer
Perched on a blazing bush of gorse.
Fishermen went laughing by,
Mallards croaked to their mates.
A swarm of midges hovered
Round our heads like a horde
Of distractions manifest,
And laughingly, we picked them from
Each other's hair and clothes.
We touched for one brief moment in springtime,
Then our paths diverged.
But the cherry blossom trees
Are as beautiful as ever
And nothing has been lost.

2. Realistic view:

The fishermen strode manfully
Through the swarming veil
Around our heads.
Not you,
You abandoned the distant woods
We had travelled fifty miles to see,
Foolishly swatting each one,
And beating hasty retreat
When numbers proved too many.
(Hardly the errant knight of old).
You did look funny waving your arms
Like a windmill
And you could hardly expect me
To be impressed.
Even I can tell a mallard
From a yellowhammer
And that's without my glasses
Let alone binoculars!

THEM

Their words slice our self esteem like sharpened
    knives.
Their cruel sarcasm mars our shattered lives.
The summer sun's rays dim in the sky.
They expose our weaknesses and make us cry.
They grind our feelings in the dirt,
And gain amusement from our hurt.
We are alone, lost sad.
They are wicked, evil bad.

TEDDY BEAR

Soft and warm, honey coloured bear,
You, my friend, are always there.
They don't care,
They don't share,
I'll hide my tears in your cosy hair.
Yes I will conceal my grief.
You have no heart, you feel no pain,
Your lack of life is my gain,
Your stillness, my relief.

ANOTHER GLASS OF WINE?

Hatred screws you up.
We spend our time
In crafty machinations,
Combining with each other,
Weaving intricate webs of cunning
To ensnare the victim.
And when we have decimated
That one's sense of importance,
Gleefully we congratulate ourselves,
Pour another glass of wine.
But the taste of victory is bitter,
The party is an empty sham
Concealing menace.
And I begin to suspect
I'm next on the hit list
So I cover my tracks with care.

YOU

I put a smile on yesterday,
I wore it just for you;
I fixed it in the mirror,
You said it would not do.

I bought a new dress last week,
I even curled my hair,
But when I went to show you,
You were just not there.

My eyes shone for you last month,
And my heart beat fast,
I told you that I loved you,
But I knew it wouldn't last.

Last year I passed you in the street
And you came and stole my shadow.
Tell me, did we have to meet?
And did you really need to go?

MONUMENT

Our love
Is like an earthworks
Curious sightseers view
To dream of a glorious past.

You said our love
Would be a monument
We'd place upon a hill
A beacon for the lonely,
Lantern of hope for shipwrecked sailors.

But you did not say
The rain and wind would come,
Our fortress fall
To first invaders.

And now our love
Exposed on a barren windswept hill
Is an empty ruin,
Visited only by grim-faced historians.

Could we resurrect it please?

ONCE I WAS ABLE TO SIT UPON YOUR KNEE

Once I was able to sit upon your knee,
Lean against your soft sparkling cardigan,
Feel your strong arm gently supporting me
As my tiny fingers explored your face,
Time's secrets line-mapped there,
A life to trace.
Your bright azure eyes shone like a jewel,
We were together in a timeless place.

But memories of shimmering summer days
Fade like the horizon's indistinct haze,
Through mocking echoes, voids of empty space.
This material world is very cruel.
How could I know you would become so small?
So that now you are hardly there at all.
Soon I know your spirit will soar free
But once I was able to sit upon your knee.

DAD

Now that you have gone
There is an empty space cut-out
That pervades my vision.
A piece of the world's jig-saw is missing,
And I cannot find you.

Once you walked across the sand
But the waves erased your footsteps.
You joined us at this table,
Your place is no longer set,
You spoke of all your hopes and plans
Until your voice was silenced,
Your body became your prison,
And you slowly faded from our view.

You gave me life, and love and joy,
But time was eclipsed for you
And there's a void left
Now that you have gone.

THE PURPLE BAMBOO PARK
(A GLIMPSE OF HEAVEN)

Long long ago in a flower forest far away
I glimpsed a view of heaven;
And I stood transfixed
In a tapestry of perfection
Surrounded by verdant growth
And vibrant tropical flowers
As the exotic birds and insects fluttered
Through the shimmering heat
And the distant waves lapped,
Gently caressing the palm fringed coral sand.

The bustling noise, crowds and dust
Of a busy Chinese street,
Little prepared me to be transported
Once more into this parallel universe.
But beyond the gates of the Purple Bamboo Park
Peace completely surrounded us,
Time seemed suspended
Like a bubble in a paperweight.
And space expanded unfolding
In infinite vistas.
We saw a tiny caterpillar
Suspended on a silken thread
Which began to spin its cocoon
And slowly ascend back up
To its bamboo branch,
And a pair of dragonflies
Were locked together

In a love-embraced flight,
As our boat drifted through
The trailing lotus blossoms
Into the serenity of loveliness.

And I pictured myself, Ophelia-like,
Wreathed in flowers
Transported into an Impressionist painting.
And I felt once again at peace,
My spirit healed.

THASSOS

Out of the blue the paraglider swooped
Like an avenging angel,
The failing sunlight filtered through
The olive trees
And set the distant Aegean Sea ablaze
With dancing flames
And the crickets maintained a constant chatter.

ANIMAL FARM

Have you ever felt like no one,
Just a tiny puff of air,
When everyone surrounds you
And you are just not there?

And have you ever felt the foreboding,
That leaden sense of dread
As the accusing finger
Slowly settles above your head?

They decimate your sense of worth
They destroy your pride,
They disregard your efforts
Until you want to hide.

They criticise and analyse
From their pedestal so high,
They microscopically examine you
And eventually make you cry.

Their cruelty knows no limits
Yet they have no sense of shame,
God urges us to forgive
But they have you in the frame.

Have you ever felt
Unable to eat, laugh or sleep
As though they have stolen your soul
So you can only weep?

And have you ever felt like no one,
Evaporating into the air
When hatred surrounds you
And you wish you were not there?

(Power corrupts and absolute power corrupts
   absolutely)